This book is intended to provide general guidance on the law in England. It does not constitute legal advice and is not an authoritative treatment of the law. Professional advice should be sought before acting on any of the material contained in this book as it may not be appropriate to your circumstances. This book is not intended to be used in place of reading the Codes of Practice or the Equality Act.

This book is available free to download in PDF format from:

http://www.inclusivechoice.com/ParentBook.pdf

I0462381

4th Edition

© Inclusive Choice Consultancy 2017

ISBN 978-0-244-33753-7

www.inclusivechoice.com

A parent's guide to disability discrimination and their child's education

Contents

About the author

Inclusive Choice Consultancy's director is Geraldine Hills. Geraldine has been working with people with disabilities for many years in various capacities. She has experience of the Special Educational Needs and Disability Tribunal (SEND) process both as a volunteer for the Independent Parental Special Education Advice (IPSEA), and as a parent who successfully won a tribunal case for her disabled child.

She has qualifications in teaching adults, and holds a BA in Learning Disability Studies from the Victoria University of Manchester. She lectured at Manchester University in Disability Education Law, and has carried out post-graduate research projects at the university.

Geraldine is the author of several books which can be found on Amazon and on the Inclusive Choice Consultancy website. She is a qualified trainer and runs many courses for Manchester City Council as well as other local authorities. You can find out more about her courses and book at www.inclusivechoice.com

Acknowledgements

I would like to thank Leslye Vaughan for her contribution to this book, writing the Education Health Care Plan chapter.

Leslye has worked for many years in the disability field and has a vast knowledge-base on subjects including autism and the EHCP to name a few. She also works with parent groups providing support and guidance to those that need it. Leslye is also a volunteer on the Parent Champion programme for her local authority

If you would like to find out more about Leslye and what she can offer your organisation you can find her here: Leslyevaughan@hotmail.co.uk

Foreword

This book is for you to use in whatever way you need to use it. You may need a better understanding of the Equality Act (2010) and the Disability Discrimination laws that are part of it. You may want a better understanding of how the Equality Act relates to your child within the education system or you may need to compose a letter to your school about the educational treatment your child is receiving.

This book is designed to support parents in their understanding of the Equality Act (EA) and how this relates to the successful inclusion of their disabled child in school. In particular, the book looks at and discusses the two key principles behind our disability discrimination laws, which are "Less Favourable Treatment" and "Reasonable Adjustments" and how this works in relation to special educational needs in education.

Most of all I have written this book to help parents build a stronger partnership with their child's school and to provide them with the knowledge necessary to challenge schools in relation to their child's education.

Words and terms

Throughout this book, the term Education Health Care Plan (EHCP) is used to replace the old term "Statement". On the 1st September 2014, transitional arrangements were put in place to support the changeover from those with statements to an EHCP.

The term 'parent' is meant as a shorthand way to say, 'parent or carer or legal guardian'.

Also, the term 'disabled' is often used to mean 'Special Educational Needs or disabled', again to make the text simpler. In some occasions, there is a legal difference between 'SEN' and 'disabled', and in this case, it is specified which term is meant.

Some parents may experience difficulties with schools. However, there may also be problems with nurseries, colleges of further education, and even universities. Again, to simplify the text, the word 'schools' is used to represent all forms of education. If there is a difference, then it will be pointed out in the text.

Introduction

I don't believe any parent sets out to create conflict, tension or misunderstanding in the lives of their child, but I do believe that the thing parents all have in common is that we love our children and strive to gain what is best for them, and what improves their life chances.

In a recent report on education for disabled children, the author mentioned the phrase 'warrior parents' to describe parents that are fighting for their disabled child's education. Failures by schools to comply with what the law demands of them can cause a situation where parents of children with disabilities are seen as "the problem". As a result, parents lose confidence in the schools. As the system stands it often creates 'warrior parents'. The parent feels there is a need to fight which often put them at odds with the school and Local Authority (LA). This in turn can create a climate of mistrust and conflict from both parent and professional alike.

I don't think of myself as a 'warrior parent'. I don't like the term "warrior parent" as to me it implies I am going to 'war', fighting and creating conflict. This is not the case; as a parent I am determined and bound to do the very best I can for my child and to make sure that he gets a fair chance, as any other child would in their education.

Would it not seem strange to read that after years of nurturing a child a parent does not teach that child road safety, or how to survive in the adult world? We all have feelings of wanting to protect our children from every possible perceived danger or wrong-doing towards them, yet we do not hear the term 'warrior parent' when it comes to mainstream parents if they challenge any issues surrounding their child's education.

Conflicts often arise between parents and schools because parents feel they have a lack of involvement. It does not have to be like this. I have experienced winning a tribunal case against a school because of their discriminatory practices against my disabled son. I do not regret taking the stance I did for my child and I would do it again if I had to, but I would urge any parent to try to resolve any issues they have with a school at a local level before they do anything else.

As parents, we have a much clearer understanding of our child's disability. Even though our children spend a large part of their time in school, this doesn't mean that the school will fully understand what reasonable adjustments might look like for your child. This is why it is very important that we work in partnership with schools and offer our support as much as possible, because it is the best way that we can be sure that the school is meeting the needs of our child.

Jargon busting

Acronyms are sometimes used to exclude people by talking in a way that only some people know what is being said. If we want to be inclusive then we need to use inclusive language that everyone can understand. I try to use acronyms and jargon as little as possible; however it is inevitable that they will be used in everyday conversation in this area, and so I present their definitions right here at the start…

EA	Equality Act
EHCP	Education Health Care Plan
SEND CoP	Special Educational Needs and Disability Code of Practice
EASS	Equality Advisory Support Services
SEND	Special Educational Needs and Disability (Tribunal)
IPSEA	Independent Parental Special Education Advice
IAS	Information Advice Services
EHRC	Equality and Human Rights Commission
LA	Local Authority
Statutory	Required by law

The Equality Act 2010

In 2010, the Equality Act was introduced to organise and collect together the complicated and numerous array of Acts and Regulations, which formed the basis of anti-discrimination law in Great Britain, for example, the Sex Discrimination Act, the Race Relations Act, and the Disability Discrimination Act.

The Equality Act defines eight "Protected Characteristics" for people who use services. These are:

1. Age
2. Disability
3. Gender reassignment
4. Marriage and civil partnership
5. Pregnancy and maternity
6. Race
7. Religion and belief
8. Sex (gender)
9. Sexual orientation

This book only describes the legislation governing disability.

Definitions of disability and SEN

Disability

In the Equality Act, "Disability" is defined as follows:

> "A person has a disability for the purposes of this Act if he has a physical or mental impairment which has a substantial and long-term adverse effect on his ability to carry out normal day-to-day activities."

There is a common misunderstanding that the EA covers only people who have a sensory or physical impairment. The breadth of the EA definition arises from the breadth of the terms:

- Substantial, defined as *"more than minor or trivial"*
- Long-term, defined as *"a year or more"*.

The definition includes a wide range of impairments, including hidden impairments. If, for example, a child has an impairment affecting their mobility, sight or hearing, or has learning difficulties, mental health problems, epilepsy, autism, a speech and language impairment, asthma, diabetes or HIV, then they may have a disability if the effect of the impairment on the child's ability to carry out normal day-to-day activities is 'substantial' and 'long-term'.

The test of whether the impairment affects normal day-to-day activity is whether it affects one or more of the following: mobility; manual dexterity; physical co-ordination; continence; ability to lift, carry or otherwise move everyday objects; speech, hearing or eyesight; memory or ability to concentrate, learn or understand; or the perception of risk of physical danger.

Questions often arise about whether children with behavioural difficulties are included in the definition. A child may have significant behavioural difficulties and these may relate to an underlying impairment. If they do, the child may count as disabled because of the underlying impairment.

The EA also covers people with:

- Severe disfigurements
- Impairments which are controlled or corrected by the use of medication, prostheses, or other aids (excluding spectacles)

- Progressive symptomatic conditions
- A history of impairment
- Cancer, HIV or multiple sclerosis.

The EA does not cover addiction to or dependence on nicotine, tobacco or other non-prescribed drugs or substances; hay fever; or certain mental illnesses, which have anti-social consequences. It is possible for a child to have special educational needs, but not be disabled for the purposes of the EA, and vice versa, although the majority of disabled children will also have some special educational needs. Figure 1 shows this.

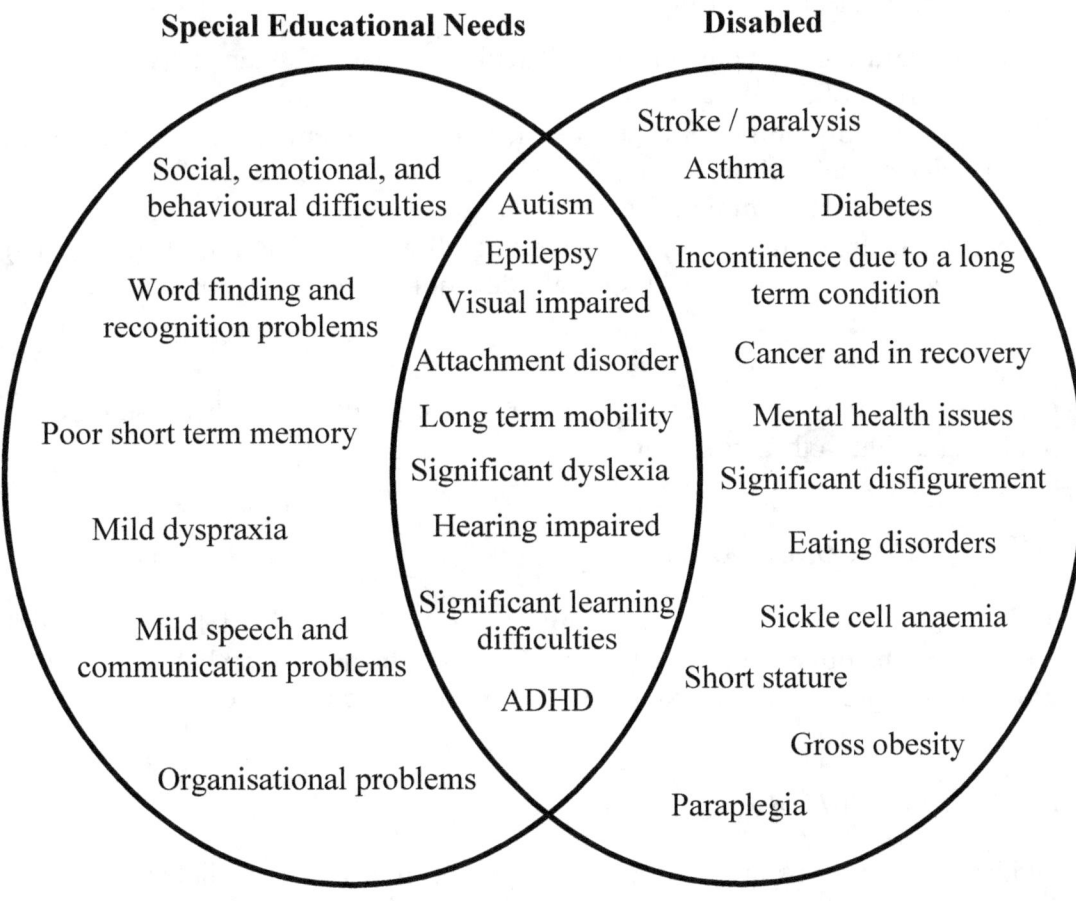

Figure 1

Special Educational Needs (SEN)

Not all children who are defined as disabled will have SEN. For example, those with severe asthma, arthritis or diabetes may not have SEN but may have rights under the EA. Similarly, not all children with SEN will be defined as having a disability under the Equality Act.

The Department for Children and Families defines children with SEN as:

> "Having learning difficulties or disabilities, which make it harder for them to learn or access education than most other children of the same age."

Children have a learning difficulty if they:

- Have a significantly greater difficulty in learning than the majority of children of the same age; or
- Have a disability which prevents or hinders them from making use of educational facilities of a kind generally provided for children of the same age in schools within the area of the Local Authority
- Are under compulsory school age and fall within the definition at (a) or (b) above or would so do if special educational provision was not made for them.

Children are not regarded as having a learning difficulty solely because they are not being taught in their first language.

SEN, Disabled, or both?

Though the definition of disability comes from the EA and the definition of SEN comes from the Education Act 1996, there is a significant overlap between the two groups of children. A child may fall within one or more of the definitions.

Hidden impairments

Hidden impairments are those, which might not be immediately obvious. However, they are also covered under the definition of disability. Examples include:

- Attention Deficit Hyperactivity Disorder (ADHD)

- Dyslexia
- Autism
- Physical co-ordination
- Incontinence
- Ability to lift, carry or otherwise move everyday objects
- Speech, hearing or eyesight (unless correctable by spectacles)
- Memory or ability to concentrate, LArn or understand;
- Perception of risk of physical danger

Disability discrimination - how the law works

Types of discrimination

What you are reading below is law and education and employers must not break these laws (and you have a right to challenge any organisation if you feel they have broken them). These forms of discrimination are defined in the Equality Act:

- Direct discrimination
- Discrimination arising from disability
- Indirect discrimination
- Discrimination by harassment
- Discrimination by victimization
- Discrimination by association
- Discrimination by perception

The meaning of each of these is as follows:

Direct Discrimination

This is discrimination directly related to the child's disability itself. For example, not allowing a child with a disfigurement to appear in a play because of their looks.

Discrimination arising from disability

This is discrimination for a reason connected to the child's disability. For example, a nursery requiring all children to be toilet trained before being admitted to the nursery may discriminate against a child with a disability that causes them not to have full bowel control. Discrimination arising from disability has occurred when a disabled child is treated:

- less favourably than someone else;
- for a reason related to the child's disability;
- when it cannot be justified.

Indirect discrimination

This is when a school or nursery put in place rules, policies, or practices which apply to all children, but which particularly disadvantage disabled children.

Discrimination by harassment

Harassment occurs if you engage in unwanted behaviour which is related to a child's disability, and which violates the child's dignity, or creates an intimidating, hostile, degrading, humiliating or offensive environment for the child. We will look at this in more detail on page 24.

Discrimination by victimization

Victimisation is treating someone badly because they are making a discrimination claim, or helping someone else make a claim. We will look at this in more detail on page 24.

Discrimination by association

This is when discrimination occurs because of a victim's *association* with a child with a disability. We will look at this in more detail on page 23.

Discrimination by perception

This is when a non-disabled child is discriminated against because the school or nursery *wrongly believe* them to have a disability, and they are treated less favourably because of that belief. We will look at this in more detail on page 23.

Remember, in practice it is not important to know the 'name' of the type of discrimination; it is enough that you might think your child has been discriminated against.

Discrimination duties

Discrimination has taken place if:

- a child is treated less favourably than someone else, because of their disability; or
- a child who is disabled is placed at a substantial disadvantage because reasonable adjustments have not been made to take account of their disability.

The equality act makes it illegal to discriminate against a disabled child for a reason related to their disability. It also makes it illegal to have rules, policies, or practices which apply to everyone but which particularly disadvantages disabled children. Schools and nurseries must make "Reasonable Adjustments" to allow disabled children to take part in all of the school or nursery activities.

These requirements can be summed up by two duties:

Less Favourable Treatment

Disabled children are entitled not to be treated less favourably than non-disabled children for a reason relating to their disability, without justification.

Reasonable Adjustments

Disabled children are entitled to have reasonable adjustments made with respect to admission arrangements or in the provision of education and associated services, to prevent them being placed at a substantial disadvantage, without justification.

These duties do not mean that disabled children have an excuse for disruptive or anti-social behaviour. There must be a direct relationship between the reason for the less favourable treatment and the child's disability.

Less Favourable Treatment

Disabled children are entitled not to be treated less favourably than non-disabled children for a reason relating to their disability, without justification. Less favourable treatment is judged to have occurred when a disabled child is treated...

- less favourably than someone else;
- for a reason related to the child's disability;
- when it cannot be justified.

This is best understood with examples:

1. A parent seeks admission to a school nursery for her child who has a bowel disease. The nursery says that they cannot admit him until he is toilet trained - that is their policy for all children. Some bowel diseases may add to the late establishment of bowel control. The refusal to admit the child is for a reason related to his disability and may be discriminatory. There may sometimes be justification for less favourable treatment, but it is the blanket policy in this example that is likely to make it discriminatory.

2. A pupil with autism goes to the front of the dinner queue. A teacher standing nearby tells him not to 'barge in'. The pupil becomes anxious but does not move. The teacher insists that the pupil must not 'jump the queue'. The pupil becomes more anxious and agitated and hits the teacher. The pupil is excluded temporarily from the school.

   a. Was there any less favourable treatment?

   b. Is the less favourable treatment for a reason related to the pupil's disability?

The reason for the exclusion was hitting the teacher but this may be related to the pupil's disability. Particular features of his autism may be that he has difficulty in managing social situations, he has difficulty in understanding the purpose of a queue, he has difficulty in understanding figurative language, such as 'barge in' and 'jump the queue,' or he has difficulty in managing escalating levels of anxiety. If the hitting is related to these features of his autism, then the less favourable treatment, the exclusion, is for a reason related to the pupil's disability and the school may well have discriminated against him.

Case study 1

A girl with Tourette's syndrome is admitted to a school. The school wants her to have all her lessons in a separate room in case she might distract or frighten other children with her involuntary noises and body movements.

The reasons for placing the pupil in a separate room are the involuntary noises and body movements. These are an intrinsic part of her disability.

The school also claim that the inclusion of the pupil is causing significant disadvantage for the provision of efficient education for other children.

1. **Is the less favourable treatment related to the child's disability?**

   The reasons for placing the girl in a separate room are the involuntary noises and body movements. These are an intrinsic part of her disability. The less favourable treatment proposed is for a reason that relates to the girl's disability.

2. **Is the less favourable treatment justified?**

   The school tries to justify the less favourable treatment on the basis that the girl might frighten the other pupils. In this case, the reason is based on general assumptions about the girl and about the other pupils and is unlikely to constitute a material and substantial reason. This is likely to be unlawful discrimination.

Case study 2

A school leave a girl behind when the rest of her group goes to the park to see a puppet show. The girl has learning difficulties and the staff consider that there is no point in taking her as she will not understand the show, and might be afraid of the puppets.

1. **Is the less favourable treatment related to the child's disability?**

   The reason for not taking the girl to the show is that she had learning difficulties. This is an intrinsic part of her disability. The less favourable treatment proposed is for a reason that relates to the girl's disability and may be discriminatory.

2. **Is the less favourable treatment justified?**

   The responsible body seeks to justify the less favourable treatment on the basis that the girl has learning difficulties and the staff consider that there is no point in taking her as she will not understand the show. In this case the reason is based on general assumptions about the girl and about the other children and is unlikely to constitute a material and substantial reason. This is likely to be unlawful discrimination.

Example

This is my own tribunal case:

South Man

Sunday, August 30, 2006

School back in dock for faili

A PRIMARY school has found itself in the dock again for discriminating against a disabled boy. The school has been ordered by a tribunal to straighten out its policies for supporting children with disabilities after it was found to have discriminated against a former pupil. One of these grounds was that the school had shown a "negative attitude" towards the child during his transition from his old special school to the mainstream school. The tribunal therefore found that the child's parents were correct in removing him from the school. Two other grounds related to the school's failure to use a home-school book which put Samuel at a "significant disadvantage" and caused "fundamental problems" with his transition placement. The tribunal also found the head had written a communique vis-a-vis Samuel's needs and suitability for mainstream education based on out-of-date reports dating back to when he was assessed by an educational psychologist at three years old.

Ren foll imp

The that rela the beh of a exp in li its beh con or v

It m tota thin dec:

The case above (my case) shows that the most important thing a school can have is the right *attitude* towards inclusion. In this case, the reasonable adjustments that the school needed to put in place were very minor, and it was only their attitude which led them into a tribunal case. In my case the school had no real defence so I won the tribunal case for my son.

Justification for Less Favourable Treatment

Even though a child may have been treated less favourably than another child the discrimination will not be illegal if the school can show that it was justified in the circumstances. Discrimination may be justified:

- when a disabled child is refused admission to a school, as a result of a 'permitted form of selection' – that is, a legal way of choosing pupils;

- because an adjustment would involve providing aids and services or removing or altering a physical feature (these are not included in the definition of reasonable adjustments a school must make);

- because of the costs and practicality of making a 'reasonable adjustment';

- because of health and safety issues.

Less favourable treatment that is justified is not unlawful discrimination. However, before schools seek to rely on a justification for a refusal of provision of services to a disabled child, they should first consider whether there are any *reasonable adjustments* (see page 15) that could be made. They need to give careful consideration as to how they include disabled children and on what criteria disabled children may be excluded from certain activities. Where a decision is taken that the exclusion of a disabled child is justified, the school will probably need to show they have consulted with other relevant professionals to look for ways to overcome the difficulty, otherwise they would leave themselves open to charges of discrimination.

Case Study 4

> An eleven-year old girl with learning difficulties applies to go to a grammar school that selects its intake based on academic ability. She fails the entrance test, and is refused admission.

1. **Was there less favourable treatment?**

    The refusal to admit the girl is based on her performance in the test. Her performance in the test is related to her learning difficulties, so this would be a case of *less favourable treatment for a reason that relates to her disability.*

2. **If so, was the less favourable treatment justified?**

    Yes.

3. **If so, why is it justified?**

    The school has operated its selective criteria without regard to the children taking the test, and the less favourable treatment is likely to be justified because it is the result of a *permitted form of selection.* This is then likely to be lawful. Only schools which are allowed to select their intake are permitted to do this however.

Reasonable adjustments

The Equality Act requires schools to make *reasonable adjustments* to ensure that disabled children are not at a substantial disadvantage. This means putting things in place that make it easier for a disabled child to join in with all the activities of the school.

Reasonable adjustments must:

- prevent disabled children being placed at a substantial disadvantage
- be aimed at *all* disabled children
- be anticipatory (they should be put in place *before* the child needs them)

The Act doesn't specify what factors should be taken into account when considering whether or not a step is a 'reasonable' one to take. It will depend on the school's size and resources, and on how the child's disability affects them.

Some of the following factors might be taken into account when schools are considering what is reasonable:

- how effective any steps would be in overcoming the difficulty that disabled children face in accessing the services
- how practicable it would be for the school to take these steps
- how disruptive taking the steps would be
- the financial and other costs of making the adjustment
- the extent of the school's financial and other resources
- the amount of any resources already spent on making adjustments
- the availability of financial or other assistance
- health and safety issues

Schools should not wait until a disabled child requires the use of their services, they should think in advance about what children with a range of impairments might reasonably need, such as children who have a visual impairment, hearing impairment, mobility impairment, or a learning disability.

Schools must also make reasonable adjustments to policies, practices and procedures that make it impossible or unreasonably difficult for disabled children to join in the full life of the school.

Schools cannot operate blanket bans on certain categories of disability. For example, they cannot refuse admission to all children with autism. If a school wishes not to accept a certain disabled child, they must demonstrate that the child's needs are such that they *cannot* be met within that school, even when all reasonable adjustments have been considered.

If a child is refused admission and the reason is felt to be justified, the schools must be aware this decision covers *only this one instance*. It does not mean the school can exclude another child with a similar disability based on the first case. They must take into consideration the specific circumstances of the individual child.

There may be times when disabled children are excluded from activities and services for reasons which are not directly related to their disability. The school should make clear to the parent of the child what these reasons are when this is the case.

Case study 3

Let's look again at Case study 2 on page 11 and think about what reasonable adjustments could have been made:

> A school nursery leaves a girl behind when the rest of her group goes to the park to see a puppet show. The girl has learning difficulties and the staff consider that there is no point in taking her as she will not understand the show, and might be afraid of the puppets.

The school does not appear to have considered how the girl might be supported in watching and enjoying the puppet show if she had accompanied the other children, or how they might have prepared her for the show. A number of possible strategies are available, including:

- Puppets played with in advance of the visit, to familiarise the girl with puppets. In real life the staff thought the girl might be afraid of the puppets and this contributed to their decision not to take her. Playing with the puppets in the nursery could help to overcome any fear;

- Finding out in advance what story is going to be told at the puppet show;

- Reading the story before the show, to familiarise the girl with the story;

- Using puppets and props to act out the story before the visit;

- Acting out the story in other ways before the visit, for example: dressing-up;

- Visiting the park beforehand to familiarise the child with the surroundings;

- At the visit itself, deploying staff so that the girl is in a small group with some of the children she knows best.

The nursery would need to have taken action like this to enable the child to participate in the visit. These types of action would not be to the detriment of any of the other children; rather it would benefit all the children.

If reasonable steps of this type could have been taken but were not, it may not be possible for the school to justify its actions.

The key to making reasonable adjustments is thinking ahead - anticipating barriers and how to remove them to enable a disabled child to be included in all school curriculum activities and benefit from it. To do this effectively it is necessary to involve parents and children in sharing information and in thinking creatively.

Examples of Reasonable adjustments and good practice

Example 1

Two hearing-impaired children are going to be admitted to a school. Some typical reasonable adjustments that the school might make include:

- Arranging training for staff in the appropriate use of hearing radio aids.
- Drawing up guidance for staff in the light of the training. This may include guidance on the use of radio microphones, the transfer of microphones to other children at group times, and checking that the children's aids are set correctly for different activities.
- Staff may decide to change the location of the book corner so that at story times and at other times when the children come together as a group, natural light illuminates the face, mouth and gestures of the staff talking to the children.
- Paying particular attention to having visual prompts to hand when they are planning activities with the children and using puppets and other props at story times.

Example 2

A small rural primary school has little experience of disabled pupils. The school is going to admit a five-year-old girl with a rare syndrome involving moderate learning difficulties, poor muscle tone, and speech and language difficulties. The head teacher consults the child's mother and a local voluntary organisation and devises a series of short training events drawing on local expertise. The training enhances staff knowledge and confidence and the girl has a positive start to school. This is likely to be a reasonable step to take to prevent the pupil from being placed at a substantial disadvantage.

Example 3

An eight-year-old boy has severe asthma. This is normally well managed. The school monitors his condition and, at the end of one term, notices that it is worse after literacy and numeracy sessions. It emerges that, at these times, he is sitting near a blackboard and the chalk dust is exacerbating his asthma. The school is concerned that the pupil might be at a substantial disadvantage. The school is in the process of replacing all the blackboards with whiteboards, and some classrooms already have whiteboards. From the beginning of the next term his class is allocated to one of the classrooms that already has a whiteboard. This is likely to be a reasonable step that the school should take

Key factors for success in making reasonable adjustments

These are examples that you may wish to discuss with your child's school and ask as to whether any of this is being implemented in the school I order to achieve successful inclusion of your child.

Vision and values based on an inclusive ethos
An inclusive vision for the school, clearly articulated, shared, understood and acted upon effectively by all, is an important factor in enabling staff to make reasonable adjustments.

A 'can do' attitude from all staff
The attitude of staff is fundamental to achieving successful outcomes for disabled pupils. Where staff are positive and demonstrate a 'can-do' approach, barriers are more easily overcome.

A pro-active approach to identifying barriers and finding practical solutions
Actively identifying barriers as early as possible and exploring solutions using a practical, problem-solving approach has led schools to identify more effective reasonable adjustments.

Strong collaborative relationships with pupils and parents
Schools that are effective at making reasonable adjustments recognise that parents and pupils have expertise about living with an impairment and will be a major source of advice. Pupils can also be the best judges of what is effective. They can be good advocates for what has worked well for them.

A meaningful voice for pupils
Schools are more likely to make effective reasonable adjustments where there are strong consultative mechanisms in place for all pupils and where peer support is well-developed.

A positive approach to managing behaviour
Combined with an appropriate curriculum and a variety of learning activities, a positive approach to managing behaviour can enable pupils to take charge of their own behaviour and support others in taking charge of theirs. Many schools

identified the importance of peer support strategies and of mentoring schemes in developing a positive approach to challenging behaviour.

Strong leadership by senior management and governors

Strong school leadership that sets a clear direction, promotes positive outcomes for disabled pupils, deploys the resources of the school to support teachers in identifying and removing barriers and keeps progress under review, makes for schools that are more effective at making reasonable adjustments.

Effective staff training and development

Where staff training and development is given a high priority it can ensure that staff have the understanding, knowledge and skills required to make reasonable adjustments for the range of disabled pupils.

The use of expertise from outside the school

Other agencies supplement and complement what a school can provide on its own. Schools may draw on a wide range of expertise beyond the school: from other local schools, units and support services; from different statutory agencies; and from voluntary organisations.

Building disability into resourcing arrangements

Building disability considerations into everything a school does, including the way it deploys its resources, enables everyone in the school to make reasonable adjustments.

A sensitive approach to meeting the impairment specific needs of pupils

A sensitive approach protects the dignity of disabled pupils, particularly in relation to meeting medical and personal care needs. Reasonable adjustments should not highlight any negative effects on the rest of the class so as to cause any resentment of the disabled pupil.

Regular critical review and evaluation

Regular reviews at pupil level, departmental level and at school level help to ensure that:

- progress is monitored;

- successes and failures are shared and inform the next steps;
- the views of pupils and their parents are sought and incorporated into the reasonable adjustments that the school makes.

The availability of role models and positive images of disability

Where schools use a range of opportunities to provide disabled role models, both children and adults, this can boost the self-esteem of disabled pupils and have a positive effect for all pupils. This can be supported by positive images of disabled children and adults in pictures, books, and a range of materials used in schools.

Case study 4

A school has received a number of complaints from local shopkeepers about the rowdy and disruptive behaviour of some of its pupils. It decides that the pupils in question should be banned from taking part in a school theatre visit because of their behaviour. One of the pupils has a hearing impairment.

1. **Was there less favourable treatment by the school?**

   The rowdy and disruptive behaviour is not directly related to the pupil's impairment. The ban from the trip may be less favourable treatment, but it is not for a reason related to the pupil's disability

2. **Can it be justified?**

   Any less favourable treatment is not for a reason related to the pupil's disability, therefore it can be justified.

Note that the 'less favourable treatment' duty does not mean that disabled pupils have an excuse for disruptive or anti-social behaviour. There has to be a direct relationship between the reason for the less favourable treatment and the child's disability.

Examples of situations schools should avoid

The following are examples of unfortunate situations which schools should avoid. They illustrate the importance of sensitivity to individual needs. Some of the inappropriate school responses described here contravene legislative requirements and could result in the school's actions being subject to challenge.

- A pupil is told off for failure to follow a long and complicated instruction given by an adult, but the pupil has speech and language difficulties and cannot process complex language.

A more appropriate response would be for the adult to make instructions short, and clarify understanding by asking the child to repeat them.

- A pupil on the autistic spectrum is disciplined for making personal comments about an adult's appearance. The pupil has no sense that such comments can be hurtful and should be avoided.

A more appropriate response would be for the adult to tell the pupil that the comment was hurtful and inappropriate, to inform the pupil's key worker or the SENCO, but not apply a sanction.

Discrimination by association and perception

The new definition of direct discrimination (see page 7) also covers cases where discrimination occurs because of a victim's *association* with someone with a particular protected characteristic, e.g. a parent or partner. Therefore, the Act would protect people who are caring for a disabled child. For example, an employer of the parent of a disabled child must make reasonable adjustments for them. Here are some examples:

> A parent of a disabled child, who has to take their child to speech therapy is harassed at work by her boss, and allowed less flexibility than other parents who do not have a disabled child.

> Ms Jones applies for a job which involves a lot of travelling. She has the best skills and experience but the company knows that Ms Jones cares for her son who is disabled. The company makes an assumption that she cannot manage because she has a disabled son and so it doesn't offer her the job. This is direct discrimination because Ms Jones is associated with a disabled person. It's against the law to refuse to offer her the job for that reason.

Protection is also provided where someone is *wrongly thought* to have a disability, and is treated less favourably because of that belief, e.g. a school mistakenly believes a potential pupil to be disabled and refuses to admit them.

Discrimination by harassment and victimisation

Harassment

Harassment occurs if someone engages in unwanted behaviour which is related to a child's disability, and which violates the child's dignity, or creates an intimidating, hostile, degrading, humiliating or offensive environment for the child. It is not necessary for the child to say that they object to the behaviour for it to be unwanted.

> Your child is a wheelchair user. When you're trying to buy something in a shop, the shop assistant makes rude remarks about wheelchair users to her colleague, which you find offensive and upsetting. You may have a claim of harassment related to disability, even though you are not disabled.

It also includes situations where the pupil is *associated* with someone who has a disability, or is wrongly *perceived* as having a disability.

Victimisation

Victimisation is defined in the Act as treating someone badly because they have done a 'protected act' (or because you believe they have done or are going to do a protected act).

A 'protected act' is:

> Making a claim of discrimination under the Act.
>
> Helping someone else to make a claim by giving evidence or information.
>
> Making an allegation that the school or someone else has breached the Act.
>
> Doing anything else in connection with the Act.

There are additional victimisation provisions for schools which extend the protection to pupils who are victimised because a family member has carried out a protected act. For example, a school must not victimise a child because their brother is the subject of a discrimination claim.

If a school does treat a child less favourably because they have taken such action then this will be unlawful victimisation. There must be a link between what the child (or family member) did and the schools treatment of them.

Information issues

Schools need information about children's disabilities in order to meet their duties. It is important that as parents we pass on information about our child's disabilities and needs so that schools can make those reasonable adjustments that are so important to the successful inclusion of our children. Also, if you do not disclose a disability to your child's school this may weaken your chances of bringing about a discrimination claim in the future. Working in partnership with the school will always be the best approach for the successful inclusion of your child.

Lack of knowledge defence

If you choose not to tell the school that your child has a disability, the school may be able to claim they did not know about the child's disability. However the school would only be able to claim this if they had taken reasonable steps to find out about the child's disability.

Confidentiality

If a parent does share information about their child's disability, but asks the head teacher to keep that information confidential, this may limit what reasonable adjustments can be made for this child. If you are requesting confidentially because you are worried how the school might react to a particular piece of information or disability then you can always take someone into a school meeting with you such as IAS, (formerly Parent Partnership) or any other type of advocate support including someone medical knowledge, or a member of your family.

Encouraging disclosure

Your support for your child's education is crucial to their progress. If your child has a disability, it is even more important that you and the school work together so your child can achieve their best, but to do this requires the school to know about your child's disability and for this you need to think about the benefits if disclosing a disability.

The school has a duty under the Equality Act 2010 (EA) to make "reasonable adjustments" for disabled children. In order to make these adjustments, the school needs to know about your child's disability.

Detailed information about the nature of your child's impairments or medical information should not be passed on unless it is relevant to making reasonable adjustments. You can request that no information is passed on to others, or you can request that information is restricted to certain people. However, you should be aware that if you do this it could limit the types of adjustments the school can make for your child. Also, if you do request that information is restricted, then this might make it difficult to bring about a claim of disability discrimination to the Special Educational Needs and Disability (SEND) tribunal because a school might claim "Lack of Knowledge".

The Disability Equality Duty

In 2005, the Disability Equality Duty (DED) legislation came into force which means it is now law. The DED is meant to ensure that all public bodies - such as central or local government, schools, Sure Start children's centres, health trusts or emergency services – pay "due regard" to the promotion of equality for disabled people in every area of their education and work.

Schools are required to write and publish a "Disability Equality Scheme" which must show how the school is meeting its general duty to promote disability equality across all its areas of responsibility.

If as a parent, you are in any doubt as to the services that your school or nursery is providing for your child, then you have a right to ask to see a copy of their Disability Equality Scheme. Within that scheme, the school or nursery should have laid out what it is currently doing to promote the achievement and well-being of its disabled children, and what more it is planning to do. If you find yourself in a situation where you do need to file a complaint then referring back to the school's scheme can be a good starting point to remind them of their duties towards disabled children.

Many schools publish their DES on their website. However, they are not obliged to put it on their website, only to publish it. If you request a copy directly from them they must supply it to you.

The disability equality duty includes two elements - a general duty and a specific duty.

The General Duty

The general duty requires schools, when carrying out their functions, to have due regard to the need to:

- promote equality of opportunity between disabled people and other people;
- eliminate discrimination that is unlawful under the EA;
- eliminate harassment of disabled people that is related to their disability;
- promote positive attitudes towards disabled people;
- encourage participation by disabled people in public life;

- take steps to meet disabled people's needs, even if this requires more favourable treatment.

The duty applies across school's duties to disabled children, disabled staff, and disabled parents, carers and other users of the school. It does not bring in new rights for disabled people, but it does require schools to take a more proactive approach to promoting disability equality and eliminating discrimination.

The Specific Duty

The specific duty requires the school to demonstrate how they are meeting the general duty. In effect the general duty sets out *what* schools have to do and the specific duty sets out *how* they have to do it, and what they need to record as evidence of what they have done. It includes a requirement to prepare and publish a Disability Equality Scheme (DES) showing how they are meeting the general duty.

The main requirements of the specific duty are to:

- prepare and publish the DES;
- involve disabled people in the development of the scheme;
- implement the scheme;
- report on it.

Code of Practice

The SEN Code of Practice is as good for parents to read as it is necessary for schools. It provides advice to schools on carrying out their statutory duties to identify, assess and make provisions for children's special educational needs. In addition, the website for this book has many other documents and booklets available for you to read. I would strongly recommend that you take a look at this. Don't think of it as a book that has to be read cover to cover but rather something you can dip into when you need to clarify something to do with your young person's education. You can down load a copy from here:

www.gov.uk/government/publications/send-code-of-practice-0-to-25

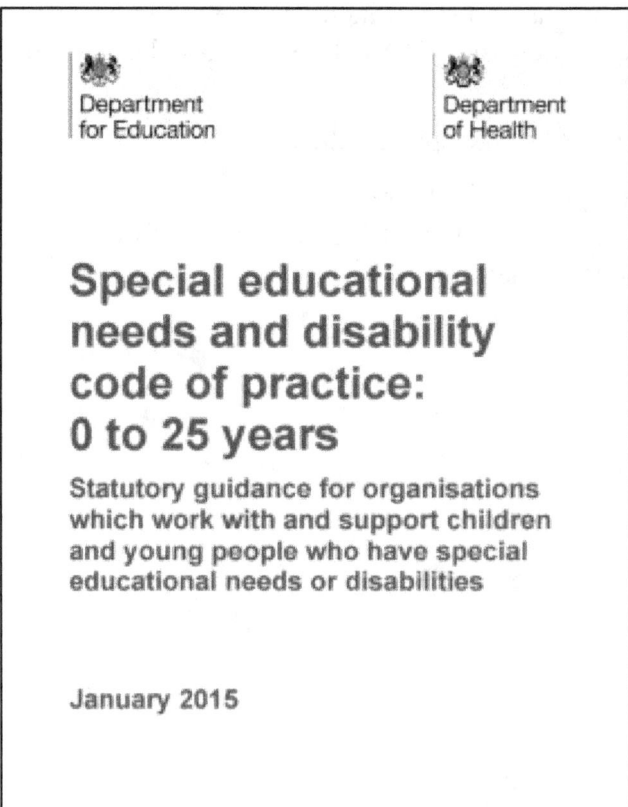

Admissions

Instances when it may not be possible to include specific children

A child or young person has a right to an inclusive education in a mainstream school or college with their typically developing peers if they want it. This can only be refused by an LA in the most exceptional of circumstances. The right to a mainstream education does not prevent a parent/young person choosing a special school/college if that is the best choice for the child/young person. It is also unacceptable for a school to refuse to admit a child thought to be potentially disruptive, or to exhibit challenging behaviour, on the grounds that the child ought first to be assessed for special educational needs.

The Equality Act 2010 prohibits schools from discriminating against disabled children and young people in respect of admissions for a reason related to their disability. Further education (FE) colleges manage their own admissions policies and are also prohibited from discriminating against disabled young people in respect of admissions. Students will need to meet the entry requirements for courses as set out by the college, but should not be refused access to opportunities based on whether or not they have SEN.

Bad practice in admissions

A SENCO reported:

> "What I've done is I've invited parents in, sometimes with the child, sometimes without the child, and I have walked them around the building. Quite fast, sometimes quite deliberately when there's a lot of movement going on and then I've just turned to the parent and said, 'do you think your child could cope with this?' So rather than say, 'no', I would say to the parent, 'do you think this is fair?' I think sometimes you have to let parents realise for themselves that this just isn't an appropriate placement".

Most people in this day and age know not to discriminate directly; however, they still make errors like this SENCO. This quotation is taken from a report published in Dec 2006 by the National Children's Bureau.

Actions such as these could result in the school finding itself in a Tribunal. This SENCO is seeing the prospective pupil as the problem - pursuing reasons why the child *can't* be included. The Act envisages that schools will adopt an approach of "what can we do to ensure that this child *is* included?"

In a large secondary school where a variety of people may show prospective students round – Year Head, Deputies etc. – it is important that everyone realises the implications of seemingly innocent actions and comments.

School Exclusions

Children with SEN and/or disabilities are much more likely to be excluded from school than their class mates. Too many children and young people with SEN and disabilities are excluded illegally. High quality teaching, differentiated for individual pupils, is the first step in responding to pupils who have or may have SEN. Schools should regularly and carefully review the quality of teaching for all pupils, including those at risk of underachievement and exclusion.

As I have discussed at the beginning of this book, schools and colleges have a legal duty to make reasonable adjustments for children and young people with SEN and/or disabilities. No matter how black a picture the school is trying to paint of your child or how many examples they give you as to why they are excluding them, they still must show that they did all they could to support your child to avoid exclusion by making reasonable adjustments.

Below are some examples of reasonable steps and adjustments to ensure that the inclusion of a child with challenging behaviour in an educational setting is not incompatible with the efficient education of others:

- Addressing factors within the class that may exacerbate the problem, for example using circle time to discuss difficult relationships and identify constructive responses.

- Teaching the child alternative behaviour, for example by taking quiet time in a specially designated area at times of stress

- Providing the child with a channel of communication, for example use of peer support.

- Using a carefully designed system of behaviour targets drawn up with the child and linked to a reward system which, wherever possible, involves parents or carers.

- Ensuring that all staff coming into contact with the child are briefed on potential triggers for outbursts and effective ways of heading off trouble at an early stage.

- Drawing up a contingency plan if there is an outburst in class, for example, identifying with the child a key helper who can be called to remove the child from the situation.

- Ensuring that if there is any possibility that positive handling may need to be used to prevent injury to the child, young person or others or damage to property, relevant staff have had training in appropriate techniques, that these have been carefully explained to the child and that the circumstances in which they will be used are recorded in a written plan agreed with and signed by the child and their parents or carers.

It is important that you and the school work together so your child can achieve their best, but to do this requires the school to know about your child's disability and for this you need to think about the benefits of disclosing a disability. Remember if you do not disclose a disability to the school or college, they may not be able to make the reasonable adjustments that could prevent an exclusion.

Types of exclusion

There are only two types of exclusion which are lawful: permanent and fixed-period. Only the head-teacher of a school (or the teacher in charge of a pupil referral unit, or the principal of an academy) can exclude a pupil. This means that legally a child is either in school full-time or they are excluded from school. Legally they can be excluded for a fixed term (for a specific number of school days) or permanently excluded (unable to return to that school unless the parent or young person can overturn the exclusion on appeal).

'Informal' or 'unofficial' exclusions, such as sending pupils home to cool off, are all unlawful regardless of whether they occur with the agreement of parents or carers. This can occur when parents are asked to take or keep them at home from school without proper notification from the school that it is an exclusion. This commonly includes picking them up from school early, at lunchtime, not coming in on certain days, or only being in school on a part-time timetable. Any exclusion of a pupil, even for a short period of time, must be formally recorded

The organisation "Independent Parental Special Education Advice" (known as IPSEA) has an excellent website for all things SEN and I would strongly recommend that you use this as your first port of call when learning more about your child's rights in education. If you go on their website for instance and search for "exclusion" in the search box then you will be taken to their exclusion page which is full of advice and printable forms for you to use to record event of exclusion so you have your own record.

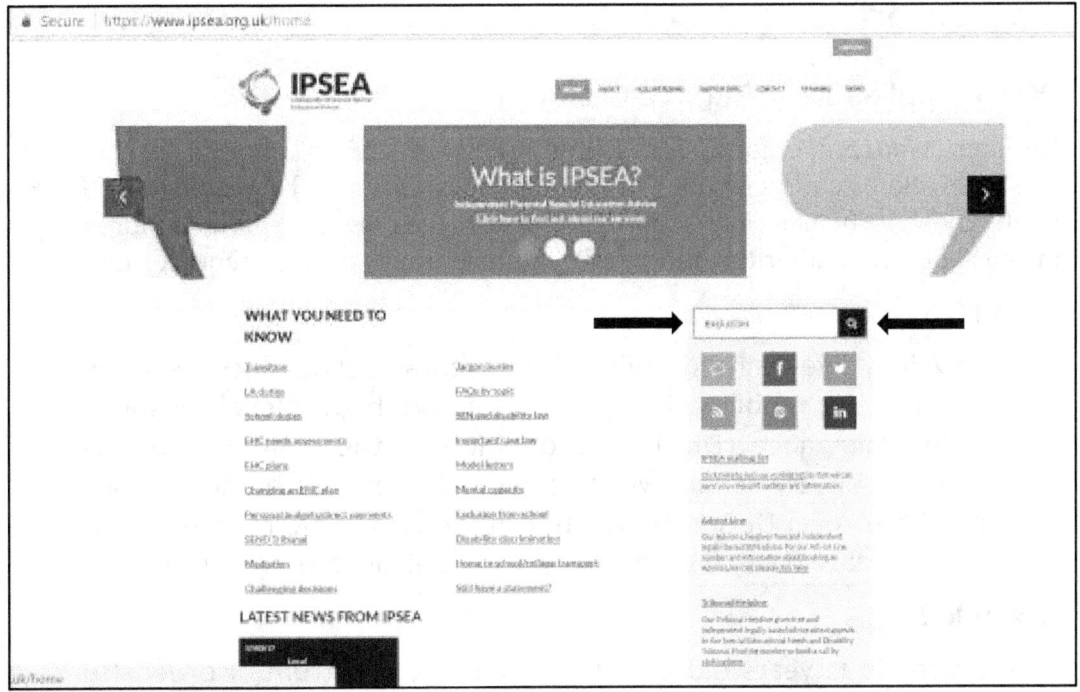

Transport

Who it applies to – "Eligible Children"

Children who are eligible for school transport are referred to as "Eligible Children". Some children with SEN and/or a disability may be unable to walk even relatively short distances to school, and this makes them Eligible Children. This means that local authorities must make suitable travel arrangements for them.

Example 1

> Lilly is a five-year-old child with cerebral palsy which severely restricts her mobility. Her parents receive higher level Disability Living Allowance (DLA) in recognition of this. Lilly attends his nearest suitable school which is one mile from her home. Receipt of higher level DLA indicates that it would not be reasonable to expect her to walk to school and so she is eligible for free transport.

Example 2

> Darren is 12 years old and has an autistic spectrum disorder. He attends his nearest suitable school which is 2.5 miles from his home. He is unaware of danger and must be accompanied even on very short journeys. Darren's doctor has confirmed that in her opinion, his carer is unable to prevent Darren from being exposed to the risks arising from his lack of awareness of danger for a journey of this length. To comply with their duty the Local Authority must ensure that suitable arrangements for Darren are in place.

Selection of school

The parents' preferred school might be further away from the child's home than another school that can also meet the child's special educational needs. In such a case, it might be open to the local authority to name the nearer school if that would be compatible with the efficient use of the local authority's resources. It would also be open to the local authority to name the school preferred by the child's parents on condition that the parents agreed to meet all or part of the transport costs.

What journeys does it cover?

The duty covers journeys to and from school at the start and end of the day, and also includes attendance at before and after-school activities.

Suitability of arrangements

For a local authority to meet their legal requirements, travel arrangements must be *suitable*. The suitability of arrangements will depend on a number of factors:

- The arrangements must enable the child to reach school without such stress, strain, or difficulty that they would be prevented from benefiting from the education provided. In a court case in 1992, the court decided that the transport provided by the local authority must be "non-stressful" if the child was to benefit from education.

- The arrangements must allow the child to travel in reasonable safety, and in reasonable comfort.

- The journey time must be reasonable. The time will depend on a number of factors, including the age and any individual needs of the child. The maximum length of journey for a child of primary school age should be 45 minutes, and for a secondary school child should be up to 75 minutes each way. A child's disability might be such that a shorter journey time is appropriate.

- Although the service needn't be a door to door service, children are not expected to walk an unreasonably long distance to catch a public service bus, or a bus journey that ended an unreasonably long distance from the school.

Arrangements could not be considered to be suitable where, for example, the child must make several changes of public service bus to get to school, which resulted in an unreasonably long journey time.

Government guidance advises on particular issues affecting pupils with severe learning difficulties and it recommends that local authorities:

- ensure drivers and escorts are known to parents

- operator contact numbers are provided for parents

- ensure stability of staffing arrangements for pupils who dislike change

- encourage schools and transport services to use a home-school liaison diary

- ensure that journey times are reasonable to avoid undue stress.

This means that local authorities will be under a duty to amend their home to school transport policy if, for example, that policy relied on disabled parents accompanying their children along a walking route for it to be considered safe, and where the parents' disability prevented them from doing so. In such circumstances, a reasonable adjustment would be for the local authority to provide free home to school transport for the children of disabled parents.

Complaints and appeals

If you disagree with a decision made about transport, you will need to start by making an appeal through the Local Authority's own internal appeals procedures. All Local Authorities should have an appeals procedure for parents to use when they have a complaint about the service or disagree with the eligibility of their child for travel support. The government's guidance "Home to School Travel and Transport Guidance 2014"

(www.gov.uk/government/publications/home-to-school-travel-and-transport-guidance)

If you are unhappy with your Local Authority's decision about your child's transport to school write to the transport section of your local council to ask for a copy of the policy and appeal procedures.

If you consider that there has been a failure to comply with the procedural rules of an appeal or if there are any other irregularities in the way the appeal was handled you may have a right to complain to the Local Government Ombudsman their website can be found at http://www.lgo.org.uk

Bad timekeeping

The service provided should ensure that your child arrives in good time for the school day. Equally your child should not be expected to leave any earlier than other children at the end of the school day (although a child may leave a few minutes early for safety reasons to avoid the end of the day rush).

The local authority's Disability Equality Duty requires them to ensure they do not discriminate against disabled people, and that all their services are planned with disabled people's needs fully considered in advance. In addition the Equality Act says that they must not provide less favourable treatment to a disabled child for a reason related to their disability. In practice this means that they must ensure that the transport arrangements do not place the child at any disadvantage over non-disabled children. If your child arrives late or is forced to leave early then this clearly places them at a disadvantage.

There is an example of a transport model letter on page 62.

Managing medicines

Parents have the prime responsibility for their child's health and should provide schools with information about their child's medical condition. We parents are a valuable resource when including disabled children, as we are often the person that knows how to deal with issues concerning our child, and we may be implementing useful practices at home that we can pass on to the school.

There is no legal duty that requires school staff to administer medicines. A number of schools are developing roles for support staff that build the administration of medicines into their core job description. Some support staff may have such a role in their contract of employment. Schools should ensure that they have sufficient members of support staff who are appropriately trained to manage medicines as part of their duties.

Positive responses by schools to a child's medical needs will not only benefit the child directly, but can also positively influence the attitude of their peers and promote positive images of disability.

It is important to inform schools about children's disabilities and any medication issues because a lack of information could be one reason a school might have for refusing to administer medication to a child. Schools need to understand why they are administering medications, the effects this might have on the child, what training needs to be in place, and what procedures already are in place at home. Without this kind of disclosure from the parent, school may be reluctant to accept responsibility for administering medications.

The policy works best where there is:

- good liaison with parents;
- good links with nursing and medical staff;
- sensitive sharing of information so that staff know the individual signs to watch for with individual children;
- a sound understanding of the pattern of a child's condition and the patterns in their treatment;
- a sound health and safety policy that includes barrier nursing.

Myth: Local Authorities have no responsibility towards children who are unable to attend school because of their medical needs.

Fact: Local Authorities must make arrangements for the provision of suitable education for children who are unable to attend school because of their medical needs. In addition, Local Authorities must not refuse or reduce such provision on the basis on how much it will cost.

The EHCP (Education Health Care Plan)

An EHCP is a legal document that describes a child or young person's special educational, health and social care needs. It explains the extra help that will be given to meet those needs and how that help will support the child or young person to achieve what they want in their life. This new legal document and process replaces the SEN Statement.

All children who have a statement will now have been transferred to the EHCP or be in the process of being transferred. All new requests for a Statutory Assessment either by school or parent referral may result in an ECHP. A statutory assessment is an investigation made by the local authorities into what the special educational needs of a child are and what provisions are needed to meet those needs but does not always lead to an EHCP being written.

Children or young people without an EHCP must not be placed in SEN Provision (such as a special school) except in very specific circumstances. Most of these exceptions require the prior consent of the child's parents or the young person over the age of 16 (other exceptions can be found in more detail on the IPSEA website).

In addition to special educational provision, the new EHCP includes health care provision and social care provision. This is a defined provision, which can be complex and misunderstood. For example, if a child or young person requires speech and language therapy, it could be assumed that this would come under the health care provision, as it is provided by the NHS. However, anything which educates or trains the child or young person must be treated as SEN provision.

Asking for a EHCP Needs Assessment

A specific request for an EHCP Needs Assessment to be carried out by a local authority may only be made by the following people:

• A child's parent;

• A young person (which, if the young person lacks mental capacity, will be the parent or other representative of the young person); or

• A person acting on behalf of a school or post-16 institution.

When should I ask for an EHCP assessment?

You can ask for an assessment at any time as a parent of a child with potential SEN. You can ask whenever a child or young person has a learning difficulty or a disability which is holding them back at school or college, and you the parent or the young person themselves believe that the school or college is not able to provide the help and support which is needed. A request should be made to the Local Authority (LA) for an Education, Health and Care (EHCP) needs assessment.

For children under 16 the parent makes the request. This includes children from 0 to 5 where parents should make a request if they believe that the child will need extra help when school starts. In the case of a young person (over 16 and up to 25) they can make the request themselves if they understand it sufficiently well – otherwise the parent can make the request on a young person's behalf.

Remember you can only ask for an EHCP needs assessment if the child or young person has or may have educational needs – it does not apply where there are only health and/or care needs no matter how severe.

Where do I send my request?

You send your request in writing or email to the Head of the LA. This person is usually (but not always) known as the Director of Education / Children's Services. You can find these details by asking the school or college, going to your local council's website. The section you need to find is called "Children's Services" or "SEN Local Offer". This is a section of your local council's website dedicated to all things regarding children's disabilities and special educational needs.

What happens next?

The LA must send a reply within 6 weeks. This reply will be sent to the parent or young person themselves, even if the request was made by the school or college and not by yourselves.

It is vital that you start keeping documents and paperwork, even copies of emails in date order in a special file. Trying using a diary to highlight the deadlines that are needed to be met by you and other professionals in this process.

The legal timelines for the EHCP needs assessments

Let's say that the local authority has agreed to carry out an EHCP assessment on your child, then they must legally adhere to certain timescales and deadlines as specified by Acts of Parliament and Codes of Practice and Regulations, see below.

TIME	LEGAL REQUIREMENT
Week 0	The request for the assessment has been made to the Local Authority, either by Educational Setting or Parents or Young Person
Week 1-6	The EHCP needs assessment begins. The LA must have gathered information and advice about the child or young person's needs within six weeks.
WEEK 12-14	A draft EHCP needs to have been produced by the LA and sent to the parent or young person by this time. Then the parent or young person can discuss with the LA about the information and contents and specifics of the draft plan. If you're not happy with the draft ask for a meeting with the LA officer to discuss the plan.
WEEK 16	The LA must contact and consult with the named provision (educational setting) on the draft plan, and that provision should respond within 15 days.
	If the LA decide not to issue an ECHP, after they have carried out assessment, they must inform the parents or young person by this date. The parent or young person will have a right of appeal.
WEEK 20	Final EHCP must be issued by this deadline.

The EHCP is a complex legal document and more details can be found on IPSEA's website.

How to complain

If you feel you are not happy with the way in which your school are behaving towards you or your child in relation to inclusion and educational provision, it is important to try and bring about a resolution at a local level first. Most complaints about schools should begin with the school's complaints procedure. By law, schools must have a procedure for parents to complain. If you cannot resolve a problem informally, for example with the class teacher, head of year, deputy head or head teacher, then ask for a copy of the procedure to inform the head and chair of governors of your concerns, and request a meeting.

Now take a deep breath and try to remember that the school may not be aware that what they are doing is discriminatory. Their behaviour maybe based on myth (what they think a particular disability might be like) or lack of correct information, or not enough information.

Your first instinct may be to go at the school blazing, but this is not the way to gain a successful outcome for your child. If it turns out that you are in the right and there has been discriminatory practice towards your child by the school, then you need to stay calm so that you can gather the information which may be necessary if you end up having to make a claim against the school.

If it turns out you were wrong, or maybe the school has acknowledged it has discriminated against your child and is willing to apologise and work towards rectifying this, then it will be difficult to work along-side them if you have been aggressive or verbally abusive.

Above all else whichever way, you choose to approach the school it is important that from day one you keep a written record of everything you do. It's no good having informal chats, as any information you tell the school, or they tell you may be lost or distorted unless it is written down clearly at the time. I would strongly advise parents that any concerns they have about the school's practices should be highlighted by a written request for a meeting, stating what your complaint is about. If the worst happens and you end up in a tribunal case, evidence is very important, since this is part of the court system. The school is likely to have plenty of written evidence, so it is important you do also.

Never go to any meeting which concerns your complaint on your own. Always take someone with you because you may be very emotional (I know I was) and you may say or do something you later regret. Also, if you take someone with you, them this person can take notes or help you should you become upset or forget what you wanted to say.

I would never recommend a tribunal case as a course of action to a parent. Tribunals are emotional, exhausting, draining and very unsettling. However, if you feel you have exhausted all avenues open to you, from written complaints, meetings and mediation, then going to tribunal may be your last remaining option. In theory, if you won, the school should apologise and put in place all reasonable adjustments and include your child correctly. In practice, much of successful inclusion is about the attitude of the school. Just because legally they are obliged to put in place certain procedures, this is unlikely to change their attitude fundamentally.

School complaints: complaining to the governing body

Most complaints about schools should begin with the school complaints procedure. By law, schools must have a procedure for parents to complain. If you cannot resolve a problem informally, for example with the class teacher, head of year, deputy head or head teacher, then ask for a copy of their complaints procedure.

Formal complaints usually end with the governing body, although some schools and local authorities may offer a further stage of complaint to the Local Authority, or access to a mediation service.

A complaint to the governing body should be addressed to the chair of governors care of the school. If the school is a community or voluntary controlled school (i.e. local authority maintained, run by the council) you could also send a copy of the letter to the director in charge of local education services, often called children's services.

In very serious cases, you could ask a solicitor to help with a letter. A solicitor might be able to add some legal points which could strengthen your case.

Try to include precise details of dates, times, meetings and decisions that may help the governing body understand the substance of your complaint. Explain what harm you or your child have suffered as a result of the school's action or inaction. Say what you would like the governing body to do to put things right, for example:

- Offer an apology
- Provide extra support for your child
- Change a school policy

The governing body is likely to pass your complaint to a panel of three or five governors. They may invite you to a meeting to put your case in more detail. They should follow the rules of *natural justice*. These say that:

- No member should have a vested interest in the outcome or any involvement in an earlier stage of the procedure
- Each side should be given the opportunity to state their case without unreasonable interruption
- Written material must have been seen by all parties.

If new issues arise, parties should be given the opportunity to consider and comment on it.

In many cases where you can complain to an outside body (SEND tribunal), you must first exhaust the school's complaints procedure before the relevant body will consider your complaint.

When you have made your complaint to school governors they should review the child's treatment, and together with the SEN Code of Practice and any other relevant documents, decide whether their school has conformed to the Equality Act. At this point you may want to remind schools that going to tribunal is likely to be very time consuming and expensive, so if you or the school have any doubts as to whether you acted correctly, admitting mistakes, apologising, and making appropriate changes is by far the best outcome for all involved.

From my own experience of having to taken a school to tribunal, I would strongly recommend that you try to resolve any issues you have with the school at this local level first.

Mediation Service

If you not happy with the school's response to your complaint there are other options you can try before you consider making a claim to a SEND tribunal. You may wish to consider mediation as an alternative way of resolving your dispute and I would advise this route first.

Manchester City Council (check your own council website for this services) provide a service called: *Information, Advice and Support* (IAS) to help you mediate. You can contact them on:

Parent Confidential Helpline: **0161 209 8356** (Monday to Friday 10am-3pm)

Email: **parents@manchester.gov.uk**

The Equality Advisory Support Services (EASS) provide a free disability mediation service. The disability mediation service offers an effective alternative route to court action, when a breach of the Equality Act may have occurred. Disability mediation uses a rights-based approach that ensures settlements are quick and effective. The focus is on changes to practices, policies and procedures. you can find more information here: www.equalityadvisoryservice.com

Although it is generally in children's best interests for their parents' complaints to be resolved at local level and at the earliest possible stage, when the issues involve schools' and local authority's legal duties to meet children's special educational needs, it is crucial that the formal processes of complaint and appeal are not side-lined by efforts at mediation. The risk is that the mediator's drive to establish a 'middle position', combined with the LA's drive to limit expenditure, will result in parents being pressured to accept an outcome which disregards their child's actual needs and their entitlement under SEN law.

The Independent Parental Special Education Advice (IPSEA) is another support service for legal advice. IPSEA actively discourages parents from going to tribunal except as a last resort, but will of course advise and support parents where needed. If IPSEA believe that the school is in the wrong, and the school still does not accept any wrong-doing, then IPSEA will provide legal representation for the parents at tribunal. You can find out more on their website: www.ipsea.org.uk

The Law Society or your local Citizens Advice Bureau may be able to provide the names of solicitors who are experienced in these matters as well.

If mediation is undertaken and no agreement is reached, a tribunal claim can still be made, as long as it is within the six month time limit outlined later.

What Can I Claim About?

The SEND tribunal service takes claims of discrimination in certain circumstances.

Admissions

Schools and local authorities must not discriminate because of a child's disability:

- In the way they decide who will get a place in schools. This includes any rules they apply when schools are 'over subscribed' (more people apply than there are places), and how they use these rules)

- In the terms on which they offer pupils a place at the school.

- By refusing to accept, or deliberately not accepting, an application from a disabled pupil for admission.

Education and associated services

A school must not discriminate in the education and associated services it provides for disabled pupils. This covers all aspects of school life and the teaching provided to pupils. It also includes what happens at lunchtime and other breaks and activities such as after-school clubs, school trips and school orchestras. (Note: Adult education provided in schools and services to parents are not dealt with by the Tribunal.)

Exclusions

It is against the law to discriminate against a disabled pupil by excluding him or her from the school because of their disability. This applies whether it is a permanent or fixed term exclusion and includes lunchtime exclusions.

But not in every case, for example:

> *Local Authority admissions appeal panels* will consider a claim of disability discrimination in the case of a child who does not have a EHCP and who has been refused a place at a Local Authority maintained school that you want your child to attend.

Independent appeal panels consider disability discrimination in relation to all permanent exclusions from Local Authority maintained schools.

If you are claiming disability discrimination in either of the above cases, you will need to contact the Local Authority for information about this.

You can complain to the tribunal if you are:

The child's birth parents, a parent includes anyone who has parental responsibility (which includes the local authority where it has a care order in respect of the child) and any person (for example, a foster carer) with whom the child lives.

You can complain against schools, nurseries and pupil referral units maintained by a local authority, independent (private) schools and academies (which includes free schools). SEND Tribunals cannot hear claims against private nurseries, unless they form part of a school, or against further education colleges. They cannot hear claims against organisations which are not schools even if they have hired or arranged to use a school's premises. If you need to make a claim against a further education college for unlawful discrimination then you must do so via to the county court. Remember is always better to seek mediation to see if you can resolve the situation before it escalates to tribunal or court.

The SEND Tribunal

This section describes the process of an alleged act of discrimination against a school, and how it may be resolved, up to and including the SEND tribunal process. The process is shown as a flow diagram in Figure 2.

As in my own tribunal case I found this process to be extremely stressful and lengthy. I did not realise at the start that a tribunal process is also time-consuming and there are strict time lines to adhere to. All this taken in to consideration, I would still do it again if I had to. You do however need to be aware that parents are expected to provide evidence to support their claim of discrimination. Preparing your claim may involve you gathering evidence to support your case which might consist of documents supporting your claim and possibly witnesses. It is important that you seek support when bring about a claim, such as IAS.

The tribunal process as it involves schools starts when a parent of a disabled child believes that the school has discriminated against their child because of the child's disability. The school should have internal procedures for dealing with parent's complaints, and this should be used first.

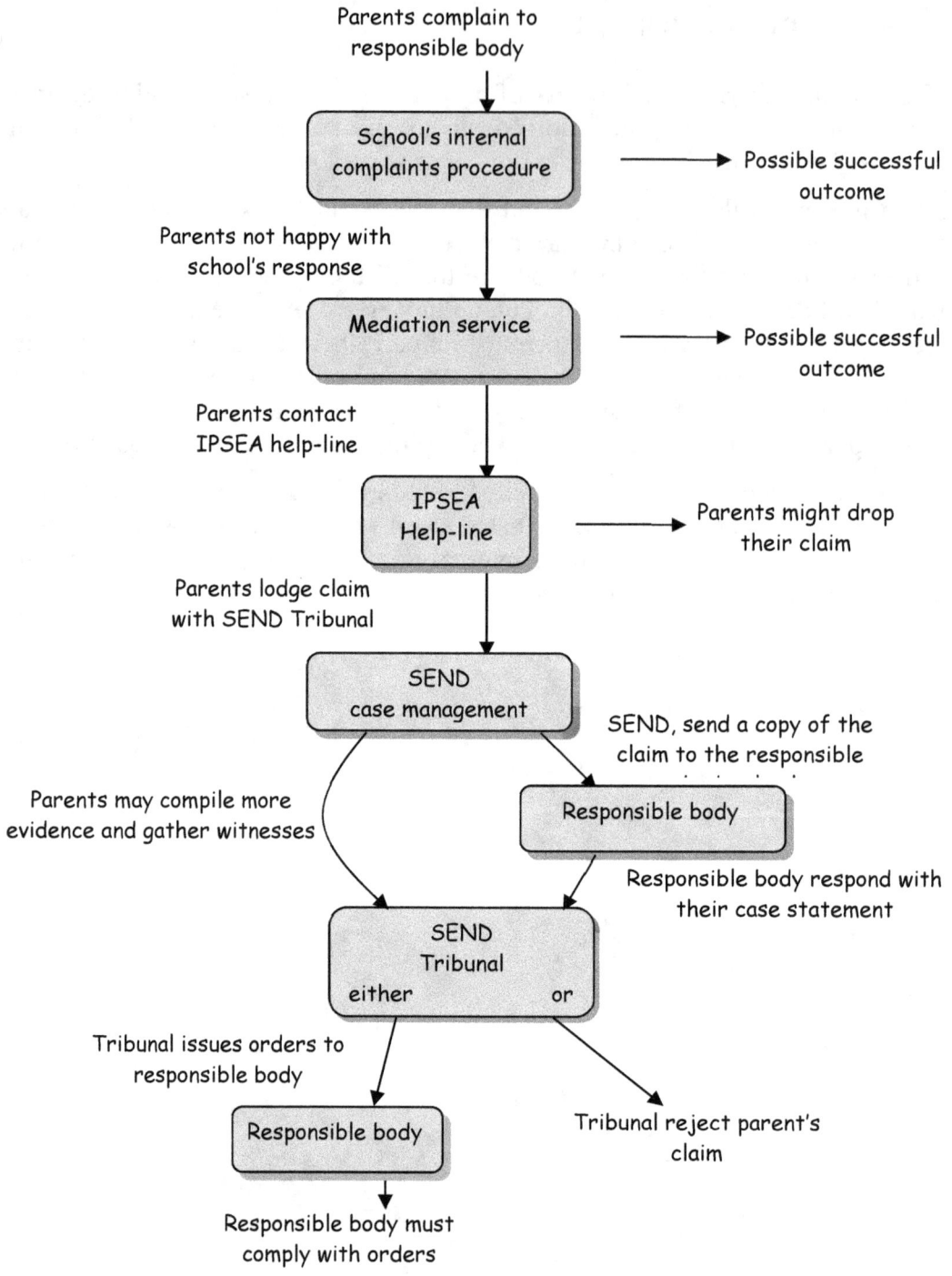

Figure 2

Some common misconceptions about the Equality Act

- ***The EA only applies to people with a physical or sensory impairment; true or false?***
  False. The EA does apply to people with a physical or sensory impairment but also to people with a wide range of other impairments, including learning difficulties and a range of medical conditions such as HIV and cancer.

- ***Alterations to improve access only apply to the physical environment; true or false?***
  False. Physical alterations are only a small part of the changes that may be needed to allow disabled people to access services. Attitudes, policies and aspects of the organisation are more likely to restrict access.

- ***Reasonable adjustments are likely to be costly; true or false?***
  False. Whilst some reasonable adjustments may be costly, most reasonable adjustments cost little or nothing.

Commonly raised issues

'Who's going to pay for it?'

Provision for individual pupils comes through the SEN framework. It usually consists of 'auxiliary aids and services' or the equipment and the human resources that are needed to support pupils who have SEN. Provision is funded by the school, from its own resources including the additional educational needs element in the school budget, and, in the case of a pupil with a EHCP, by the LA as well, though this funding is often devolved or delegated to the school. In some areas schools also have funding delegated to them for the purchase of support services.

Making reasonable adjustments is usually about how resources are used, about how schools are organised, about policies, practices and procedures. It would be a mistake to think that reasonable adjustments will automatically cost a lot.

'He can't go on the school trip. It's health and safety requirements.'

The Department for Education and Skills provides guidance on the safe conduct of school trips. This guidance emphasises the need to both:

- ensure the inclusion of all pupils: *'Every effort should be made to ensure that school journeys and activities are available and accessible to all who wish to participate…;'* and
- ensure that suitable arrangements have been put in place to ensure their safety: *'The group leader should discuss the visit with the parents of pupils with SEN to ensure that suitable arrangements have been put in place to ensure their safety.'*

Health and safety considerations are a crucial part of the planning of any school trip. They do not bar disabled pupils from participating. In line with the guidance, a risk assessment needs to be carried out for any school trip. Reasonable adjustments for disabled pupils should be part of this risk assessment. Failing to make reasonable adjustments may amount to discrimination. The Code of Practice explains how this may arise.

'Not all of these children are disabled.'

The definition of disability in the Equality Act is broad and includes many more children and young people than is normally thought. The EA says that someone has a disability if they have:

a mental or physical impairment that has a long-term and substantial adverse effect on their ability to carry out normal day-to-day activities.

Long-term means a year or more and substantial means *more than minor or trivial.* Both terms set quite a low threshold and therefore increase the number of pupils who are covered by the definition. Many pupils may not think of themselves as being disabled. Their parents may not think of them as being disabled either. That does not stop them being covered by the EA. All the pupils shown in the clips are likely to be disabled under the EA definition.

'We can't change this because of the National Curriculum.'

Integral to the National Curriculum is a statutory statement, *"Inclusion: providing effective learning opportunities for all pupils"*. This is usually known as The National Curriculum Inclusion Statement. It sets out three principles that are essential to the development of a more inclusive curriculum:

- setting suitable learning challenges;
- responding to pupils' diverse learning needs;
- overcoming potential barriers to learning and assessment for individuals and groups of pupils.

Rather than constraining what schools can do, the National Curriculum requires schools to adapt their approach to enable all pupils to access the curriculum.

'We can't take this child unless he has a full-time support assistant.'

A support assistant may be an important part of a pupil's special educational provision, but placing conditions on the admission of a disabled pupil, or potential pupil, may amount to discrimination. The Code of Practice provides examples of Less Favourable Treatment that may amount to discrimination.

'We can't take your child because of the league tables.'

Many schools find that the changes that they make for disabled pupils make the school a better place for teaching and learning. This can lead to better outcomes for all children. Many schools also focus on improving measures of pupil progress, and the value-added measures tables reflect that.

'I'm worried about the impact on other pupils.'

Many schools find that the changes that they make for disabled pupils can make the school a better place for other pupils too.

'We can't take this child. My staff are not allowed to give out medicines.'

The EA cannot require staff to administer medicines. Where staff agree to manage the administration of medicines or to administer them, schools should follow the Department for Education and Skills/Department of Health guidance, *Managing medicines in schools and early years settings*. This provides essential advice on the development of policies on the management and administration of pupils' medicines. It states clearly:

> *"Children with medical needs have the same rights of admission to a school or setting as other children. There is no legal duty that requires school or setting staff to administer medicines. A number of schools are developing roles for support staff that build the administration of medicines into their core job description. Some support staff may have such a role in their contract of employment. Schools should ensure that they have sufficient members of support staff who are appropriately trained to manage medicines as part of their duties."*

Where the administration of medicines is not in someone's contract, it is entirely acceptable for staff to volunteer to administer medicines. It may place a disabled pupil at a substantial disadvantage if a school forbids staff to volunteer.

'We can't do this without specialist support.'

Drawing on specialist support is an important part of making reasonable adjustments. Many schools draw on external expertise: to inform what they do, to train staff, to train pupils, or to provide specific advice. But specialist support is only part of the picture. Other players are important too: school staff, parents, pupils themselves.

'If we exclude the child the LA will have to do something about it.'

Exclusion is not a reasonable adjustment and would put the pupil at a substantial disadvantage. If the exclusion is for a reason related to the pupil's disability it may amount to discrimination. The Code of Practice explains the circumstances in which this may be the case. Many of the schools that have been most successful at including disabled children demonstrate a positive approach to managing behaviour and report low or no exclusions.

Appendix A: Example letters

This appendix shows some example letters that you can base your own letters on. They will need adjusting to your particular needs and circumstances. More letters may be found on the Inclusive Choice Consultancy website parent pages at...

www.inclusivechoice.com/letters.html

IPSEA also has a section with guidance and letters on their website, which can be found under here:

http://www.ipsea.org.uk

Schools' refusal to admit disabled child

Dear Sir/Madam

I wish to inform you that I am considering making an appeal against the decision not to give my child, <name>, a place at <name of school>. I would also like to make a claim under the Equality Act (2010) of Disability Discrimination. My grounds for appeal are described below.

I consider that the decision not to give my child a place was less favourable treatment of my child for a reason related to his disability and that the less favourable treatment of my child cannot be justified.

Schools have a legal duty to comply with parent's request unless they can show that either:

a) the school they want is unsuitable to their child's age, ability, aptitude or special educational needs; or

b) that their child's attendance at the school would affect the education of other children; or

c) that their child's attendance at the school would not be an "efficient use of resources."

I would like <Name of school> to put in writing:

a) Why they felt they could not meet my child's need.

b) Any evidence to back this up.

I have sought educational discrimination advice and I will be making a claim of Disability Discrimination to the Admission Appeal Panel. This is not something I wish to do so I would appreciate it if you could contact me and discuss this matter. I wish to thank you in advance and I look forward to your support and assistance in this very stressful matter.

Yours faithfully

Special education provision is not being made

Dear Sir or Madam,

Re: <Child's name> <date of birth>

I am writing as the parent of the above child, who has an Education Health Care plan and attends <school name>.

Under the Equality Act (2010), the EHCP specifies the special educational provision my child should receive and I understand that you have a legal duty to "arrange" this provision.

I am sorry to have to inform you that you are in breach of this duty, on the grounds that the following provision is currently not being made:

<Insert details here>

please reply to this letter as soon as possible, but in any event within 5 working days of receiving it, confirming the steps that you will take to ensure that the special educational provision specified in my child's EHCP will, in fact be made.

I look forward to an early reply and trust that it will not be necessary to take this matter further.

Yours sincerely,

More guidance on model letters can be found on IPSEA's website at:

www.ipsea.org.uk

Complaint that a disabled child is not included in a school club

Dear <headteacher or governor>,

I am writing concerning your school's treatment of my child, <child's name> in the <club or event>. I believe he/she was discriminated against, and I would like this situation to be rectified with immediate effect.

The Equality Act (2010) demands that in "extended services" such as this run by the school for its pupils, schools are required to make "Reasonable Adjustments" to include disabled children, and must not provide "Less Favourable Treatment". Under the act, "Less Favourable Treatment" is defined as having occurred when a disabled child is treated less favourably than someone else, for a reason related to the child's disability. In this case, it seems quite evident that you are treating <child's name> less favourable than the other children because of his/her disability.

You are required under the act to make any Reasonable Adjustments to ensure that <child's name> is included in this <club or event>. Under the act, the Reasonable Adjustments you make must act to prevent disabled pupils being placed at a substantial disadvantage, must enable pupils to participate in education and associated services, and must be anticipatory. I would appreciate your co-operation in this matter by fully including <child's name> in the <club or event> with no pre-conditions and with immediate effect, as is your statutory duty.

Thank-you very much.

Your sincerely,

Detention is being used as a form of punishment for a disabled child

Dear head-teacher or governor,

I am writing concerning your school's treatment of my child, (name)

I am concerned that the school is using detention as a form of punishment to incidents that happen in school that are directly related to my child's disability <name of disability>. My child has been officially diagnosed with <disability>. Therefore, he has protection under the Equality Act 2010.

The Equality Act demands that schools are required to make "Reasonable Adjustments" to include disabled children, and must not provide "Less Favourable Treatment". Under the act, "Less Favourable Treatment" is defined as having occurred when a disabled child is treated less favourably than someone else, for a reason related to the child's disability. In this case, it seems quite evident that you are treating <name> less favourably than the other children because of his/her disability, in that you are imposing detention on him for a reason that is directly related to his/her disability.

You are also required under the act to make any Reasonable Adjustments to ensure that <name> is included in all activities. Under the act, the Reasonable Adjustments you make must act to prevent disabled pupils being placed at a substantial disadvantage, must enable pupils to participate in education and associated services, and must be anticipatory. I do not feel that <name> is being fully included in school life and I would very much like to work alongside you to improve things for (Name)

I would like to request a meeting with the school as soon as possible so that we can discuss what reasonable adjustments the school has/can make thus ensuring (Name) is progressing and achieving in his school environment and to offer my support as the parent to the school.

please note that I have copied this letter to the chair of governors.

Thank-you very much,

Yours sincerely,

Failure to provide school transport

Dear *<head of transport at LA>*,

I am writing to you to complain that my child, *<name>* has not been provided with transport to and from his/her school *<school name>*. *<child name>* has a disability, *<disability name>* which means he/she cannot walk very far. The school is approximately *<distance>* away so without transport he/she cannot access his/her education.

The local authority's Disability Equality Duty requires you to ensure you do not discriminate against disabled people, and that all your services are planned with disabled people's needs fully considered in advance. In addition the Equality Act (2010) says that you must not provide less favourable treatment to a disabled child for a reason related to their disability. Your decision not to provide transport has placed my child at a substantial disadvantage compared with his/her peers, and therefore you are currently in breach of the Equality Act.

Therefore, I request that you re-consider your decision, and put in place transport arrangements for my child as soon as possible.

Yours sincerely,

Bullying of a child with disabilities

Dear Sir or Madam,

Re: <Child's name> <date of birth>

I am writing as the parent of a disabled child, who attends <school name>.

I am afraid to have to complain about the fact that my child is being bullied while they are attending your school. This is causing them considerable emotional distress as well as effecting their willingness attend school.

Within the Equality Act there is also the Public Sector Equality Duty.

The Duty has three aims. It requires public bodies to have due regard to the need to:

- Eliminate unlawful discrimination, harassment, victimisation and any other conduct prohibited by the Act;

- Advance equality of opportunity between people who share a protected characteristic and people who do not share it;

- Foster good relations between people who share a protected characteristic and people who do not share it.

I am sorry to have to inform you that you are in breach of this duty, on the grounds that my child is constantly being bullied and harassed and therefore making it virtually impossible for them to foster good relationship with others.

Please reply to this letter as soon as possible, but in any event within 5 working days of receiving it, confirming the steps that you will take to ensure the bullying stops and my child feel reassured and safe to attend school

I look forward to an early reply and trust that it will not be necessary to take this matter further.

Yours sincerely,

IPSEA advice line

The IPSEA Advice Line provides legally based information and next step advice on any educational issue that is the result of your child's special educational needs or disability. Our appointments last up to 30 minutes and our advisers will give you up-to-date information on the law, explain what it allows you to do and give you clear next-step advice.

All available appointments for the next week can be booked on their website at https://database.ipsea.org.uk/book/al.

If you have any problems using the booking system, you can email bookings@ipsea.net or phone 01799 582 030.

www.ingramcontent.com/pod-product-compliance
Lightning Source LLC
Chambersburg PA
CBHW060011210526
45170CB00017B/2311